Exploring Earth's Resources

Using Plants

Sharon Katz Cooper

www.raintreepublishers.co.uk
Visit our website to find out more information about **Raintree** books.

To order:
☎ Phone 44 (0) 1865 888112
🖹 Send a fax to 44 (0) 1865 314091
🖥 Visit the Raintree Bookshop at **www.raintreepublishers.co.uk** to browse our catalogue and order online.

First published in Great Britain by Raintree, Halley Court, Jordan Hill, Oxford OX2 8EJ, part of Harcourt Education.
Raintree is a registered trademark of Harcourt Education Ltd.

Editorial: Isabel Thomas, Sarah Chappelow and Vicki Yates
Design: Michelle Lisseter
Picture Research: Erica Newbery
Production: Duncan Gilbert

Originated by Modern Age
Printed and bound in China by
   South China Printing Company

10 digit ISBN 1 406 20619 9
13 digit ISBN 978-1-4062-0619-7
11 10 09 08 07
10 9 8 7 6 5 4 3 2 1

British Library Cataloguing in Publication Data
Cooper, Sharon Katz
  Using plants. – (Exploring Earth's resources)
  1. Plants – Juvenile literature
  I. Title
  333.9'53

  ISBN – 13: 9781406206197
  ISBN – 10: 1406206199

A full catalogue record for this book is available from the British Library.

Acknowledgements
The publishers would like to thank the following for permission to reproduce photographs: Action Plus p. 17 (Glyn Kirk); Alamy pp. 14 (Visions of America, LLC), 15 (Tom Tracy Photography); Anthony Blake Photo Library p. 13; Corbis pp. 5 (Matt Brown), 7 (Louie Psihovos), 8 (Zefa/Theo Allofs), 12, 13 (Nik Wheeler), 17, 18 (Walter Hodges); Eye Ubiquitous p. 16; GeoScience Features Picture Library p. 9; Getty Images pp. 4 (Jan Tove Johansson), 21 (Stone/John Humble); Harcourt Education LTD p. 22 (Tudor Photography); Masterfile pp. 11 (Peter Christopher), 20 (Lloyd Sutton); Photolibrary pp. 6 (Frithjof Skibbe), 10 (Botanica); Science Photo Library pp. 17 bottom left (Pat & Tom Leeson), 17 bottom right (Will & Deni Mcintyre); Science Photo Library P. 19 (Philippe Psaila)

Cover photograph reproduced with permission of Corbis.

Every effort has been made to contact copyright holders of any material reproduced in this book. Any omissions will be rectified in subsequent printings if notice is given to the publishers.

Contents

Some words are shown in bold, **like this**.
You can find them in the glossary on page 23.

What are plants?

Plants are living things.

They use sunlight to make their own food.

Plants are **natural resources**.

Natural resources come from
the Earth.

Do all plants look the same?

There are many different types of plants.

Some plants have colourful flowers.

Some plants grow quickly and some grow slowly.

Some plants are tiny, like violets. Some plants are huge, like trees.

Most plants grow on land.

Some plants live in shallow water.

There are plants that grow on
other plants.

What do plants need to grow?

All plants need water and light.

Some plants need a lot of sun.
Others grow best in the shade.

Most plants need soil to grow in.

All plants need **carbon dioxide** from the air.

How do we use plants?

We eat some plants.

Farmers grow many different fruits and vegetables.

cinnamon

Spices come from plants.

We use spices in cooking. This spice is cinnamon.

We use plants to make furniture and build houses.

Workers cut down trees to make them into planks of wood.

paper

We use wood from trees to make paper.

We use wood from trees as fuel, too.

Many people burn wood to make fires for heat and cooking.

Cotton comes from a plant.
We use cotton to make clothes.

We also use plants to make
many **medicines**.

Who studies plants?

Foresters are scientists who study forests.

They decide which trees we can cut down without running out.

Other plant scientists help farmers grow healthy crops.

Will we ever run out of plants?

Plants usually grow back. They are **renewable**.

But if we use plants too quickly, we may run out before they can grow back.

To use plants more slowly, we can **recycle** paper.

We can find new uses for old wood.

Plants quiz

Take a look around your house or classroom. Can you find ten things that are made from plants?

Glossary

 **carbon dioxide** a gas that plants need to breathe

 **forester** a scientist who studies forests

 **medicine** something that helps people get better if they are sick

 **natural resource** a material from the Earth that we can use

 **recycle** re-use something that has already been used

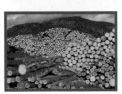 **renewable** something that will not run out

Index

Titles in the *Exploring Earth's Resources* series include:

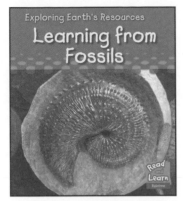

Hardback   1-406-20623-7

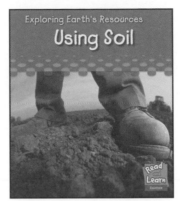

Hardback   1-406-20618-0

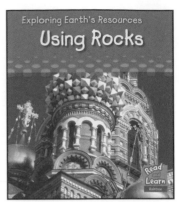

Hardback   1-406-20617-2

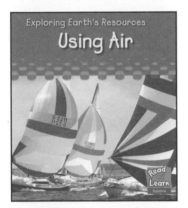

Hardback   1-406-20621-0

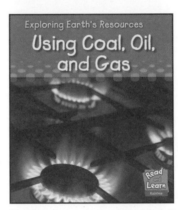

Hardback   1-406-20622-9

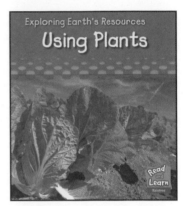

Hardback   1-406-20619-9

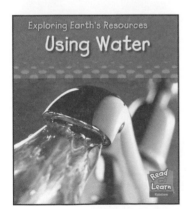

Hardback   1-406-20620-2

Find out about the other titles in this series on our website www.raintreepublishers.co.uk